STANLEY GIBBONS GUIDES

PHILATELIC EXHIBITING

Roy A. Dehn

STANLEY GIBBONS PUBLICATIONS LTD

391 Strand, London WC2R 0LX

By Appointment to Her Majesty The Queen
Stanley Gibbons Ltd, London
Philatelists

© Stanley Gibbons Publications Ltd 1978

First published 1978

ISBN 0 85259 031 8

Set in 8 on 9pt Monotype Century Schoolbook and
printed in Great Britain by Waterlow (Dunstable) Ltd

Contents

The Author

Roy Dehn, who has previously written a handbook *Italian Stamps* (Heinemann, 1973) and has had various articles published in the philatelic press both in Great Britain and in Italy, started collecting stamps in the early 1950s. He is a member of his local philatelic society and of several specialist societies as well as being a Fellow of the Royal Philatelic Society, London. He has exhibited at local, national, and international exhibitions and has been on the jury of both local and national exhibitions. His interest in collecting was originally ancillary to an enthusiasm for Italy and Italian history so, whilst he has acquired an interest in the more strictly philatelic aspects of collecting, he still retains an inclination to consider stamps and letters in the context of the social and economic history of the issuing organisation. He was for many years concerned with advertising and marketing and has therefore a professional interest in *communication*, which he believes to be one of the major obligations of the successful exhibitor.

Introduction

In May 1890, the Philatelic Society, London (which was later to become the Royal Philatelic Society, London) celebrated the jubilee of the issue of the first postage stamp, and incidentally the coming of age of the Society which had been founded twenty-one years before, by organising an exhibition in the Portman Rooms, Baker Street. The objective was to display 'a complete collection of the postal issues in all countries during the past 50 years'. The exhibition is of particular interest because it appears to have set the pattern for future international exhibitions. Significantly the exhibits were to be divided into a number of separate classes; collections of individual countries were divided from general collections, postal stationery was to be presented in two separate classes with envelopes and wrappers in one and postcards and lettercards in the other. Stamps on cover were relegated to a miscellaneous class together with essays, proofs and telegraph stamps. Of particular importance was the decision to award medals according to the merit of the exhibits.

In making this decision the committee followed the practice of the Great Exhibitions from 1851 on in which medals of differing values were awarded to manufacturers. But they might very well have thought that art exhibitions provided a better parallel and have made the qualifications for inclusion very high and refrained from making any comparative judgment between exhibits accepted for 'hanging'.

There are collectors today who regret the pattern which has been established, because they wish simply to show their collection, not to outclass their friends. Those who are of this opinion would accept the rejection by the jury of a number of badly presented collections, which is nowadays very rarely done, and believe that more space would result for the deployment of the better collections and the standard of exhibitions be raised as a result.

This is not the place to weigh the merits of the two policies, but it is right to emphasise that exhibitors at most exhibitions nowadays must accept the medal system, which has at least one important advantage. It encourages the collector to improve his collection. When collections are either accepted or rejected there is no particular encouragement to improve the exhibit before entering it at another exhibition. Where medals are awarded, however, it is possible to progress all the way from a certificate of participation to a large gold and, where progress is made, it is usually a source of satisfaction to know that an experienced jury agrees that improvements have been made.

Competitive spirits will be pleased by the prospect of having their exhibit classified, so will need no special encouragement to enter. Others may be put off by shyness or modesty. They may like to know that many of us have found that the stimulus of classification has given us the impetus to study our collections more carefully. The result has been an enlargement of our knowledge and an important increase in the pleasure we derive from our stamps and covers.

This guide has been written with this very much in mind in the hope that it will not only provide hints for improving exhibition entries but also help make the preparation of exhibits stimulating, interesting, and a source of pleasure. If the preparation of an exhibit becomes a burden, it shows on the album pages and failure to achieve the right standard of medal becomes a cause of bitterness. Juries are human and there are now so many different specialisations that it is impossible for them to be expert in them all. For this and other reasons there will always be an element of luck, particularly when an exhibit has merits which place it between two classes. This element of luck is 'part of the game' and is best accepted as such.

What is it all about?

Anyone starting a new activity is likely to find that it seems stranger than it really is. The collector who considers exhibiting for the first time may feel that there is a great gap between the ordinary collection and the exhibit. This is usually not so; and if it is so, there is probably something wrong with the presentation of the ordinary collection. Nor is the matter of exhibiting out of the way; an exhibit is simply a means of communication and in its preparation the same rules are likely to apply as do in other acts of communication, whether they involve a sales manager addressing his sales staff or a historian describing the French Revolution. The collector who exhibits is communicating to other collectors his interest and enthusiasm, showing examples which explain it, emphasising where necessary development and differences which may hold the attention of the viewer. He is 'talking about' his collection.

All this may sound very theoretical, but I suspect that more collectors fail to prepare a good exhibit because they have not thought out beforehand what they are trying to do than for any other single reason. A stamp is at one and the same time many things. For example, it is a minuscule design which can be discussed in the context of fashions in design, a piece of printing which can be discussed in terms of the technique of printing, a receipt for a rate of postage by land, air or sea, an echo of social or political history. The exhibitor will sometimes decide to give emphasis to one of these uses, sometimes to review many of them in the context of the history of the issuing country. The decision he takes will determine the theme of the exhibit.

All that used to be asked of exhibitors in the description paragraph of exhibition entry forms was the short title of the exhibit. Nowadays exhibitors may be asked to define the theme and not merely to give a 'description' of the exhibit. The rules often speak of the 'purpose' of the exhibit in much the same way as I have written of its 'theme'. So the importance of careful consideration of the objective is now incorporated in the rules themselves.

Although the methods of resolving problems are likely to be the same for both the advanced and the medium collector, their practice may differ. The first will have to consider what he can best leave out (in material and in writing-up); the second may be more concerned to discover an interesting presentation which will enable him without illogicality to use as much of his good material as possible. Both will be concerned to use their material as well as possible to illustrate their theme.

A clear definition of the purpose of the exhibit is only one side of the coin; the other side is appropriateness. Judgment on what is appropriate for a philatelic exhibition, or a section of one, is likely to vary interestingly. No one would doubt that a clean display of Penny Blacks was appropriate to the national section of a stamp exhibition, but what about Penny Blacks on cover? Nowadays their inclusion would be welcomed, but, as we have seen earlier, this would not have been so in the Philatelic Society's exhibition of 1890 when adhesives off cover were in one section and those on cover were relegated to the miscellaneous class. Postcards printed on silk might make an appropriate and attractive display in a postcard exhibition but cannot claim inclusion in a philatelic exhibition simply on the argument that they have been sent through the post. On the other hand if postal authorities decided that these cards, because of their fragile nature, needed special treatment and justified an extra fee to pay for it, then a display of these cards showing how the rates changed over the years would be acceptable, because changes in postal rates and in methods of handling if they are reflected in the stamps or markings on the cover are very acceptable. There will always be marginal cases. One of them might be provided by the interesting series of picture cards which illustrate stamps, a well known series of which was published by Ottmar Zieher of Munich. Where do these belong? I am inclined to consider that like such objects as Victorian letter balances they should not form part of the main exhibition, but should be considered very welcome side-shows.

The arguments which determine the acceptance and rejection of exhibits at a philatelic exhibition apply with equal force to the pages of the individual exhibits. Should maps be included in a postal history study? Are photographs of pilots acceptable in an air mail exhibit? The rules of almost all, if not all important exhibitions make clear that predominance must be given to the stamps or covers. Lots of photographs of pilots and few stamps or flown covers is never an acceptable mixture, any more than lots of writing-up and few stamps is. Taste and good judgment are qualities difficult to define though often easy to observe. Although they are not listed in the headings offered as guidance to judges and competitors they are likely to influence the marking. The exhibitor who strikes the right balance between the philatelic and the explanatory material should do well. The art is best learnt by trial and observation.

Commenting recently on airmail exhibits a distinguished collector who has often served on juries remarked that he was depressed at the apparent fears of exhibitors that the judges will know nothing of the subject, a fear which encouraged them to devote space to large maps of flights and times of departure to the nearest second which might better have been used to display stamps and covers. We have already discussed the importance of the right balance between material and writing up so there is no cause for disagreement here, but I think that many people would challenge the implication that exhibits should be planned to appeal to the jury. All exhibitors, I should have thought, have an obligation to plan their exhibits so that they are intelligible, and one would hope of interest, to the kind of public which is expected to come to the meeting or pass through the turnstiles. The taste of those whose sole concern is a visit to the dealers stands can, perhaps, be ignored, but the interests of those who spend time looking at the exhibits should not be. In a general exhibition the arrangement and writing-up should surely contain enough information for the collector who specialises in air mails, say, to find the collection of postal stationery intelligible and vice versa. The most pleasant compliment which can reach the ears of an exhibitor is to hear a fellow collector say: 'Now I understand why you find collecting these so interesting'.

I believe that the careful jury should be on their guard against the exhibit prepared just to please members of the jury and should give credit for the ability with which the exhibit's layout and annotation make it generally understandable. Clearly a complex and detailed study will more often be 'generally understandable' at a specialist exhibition than at a general one. What is appropriate for one may not be appropriate for the other. This has nothing to do with the quality of the exhibit. An outstanding but complex plating study may demand so much detailed attention that it is unsuitable even for a specialist exhibition and can only really be enjoyed by a single person, with a lens in hand, in the quiet of his own room. On the other hand some quite abstruse bits of philatelic research can be made interesting to the non-specialist if it is succinctly and clearly explained, and well laid out. Week-end meetings of specialist societies are becoming more popular. At these the display even of a few half-written-up sheets with tentative notes in pencil may help the work in progress.

The reader of the last few paragraphs who visits an important national or international exhibition may well encounter a number of exhibits which follow none of the suggestions so far discussed. Some of these will have been submitted by collectors of the 'old school', will display outstanding material, and will have been awarded a high prize by the judges. The reason for this is usually the quite outstanding quality of the material. Classical material in impeccable condition is always scarce and will always attract attention, even if the presentation is not the best possible and the writing-up uninformative. These exhibits warrant admiration, but are not necessarily to be copied.

Perhaps it will be useful to summarise the discussion so far in the form of a checklist. I believe that the would-be exhibitor should ask himself:

1. Have I got something to say?

2. Can I say it understandably in the space allotted to me? (Too much material can be as bad as too little.)

3. Have I the right material to demonstrate what I wish to say?

4. Is the condition of my material good enough for public display?

5. Are my material and my message appropriate for this particular exhibition (audience)?

If the answer to these questions is yes, work can start on preparing the material for display. This preparation will be discussed in more detail in the pages which follow. Here only a few general remarks are appropriate.

Very early in the history of exhibitions it was realised that, if the value of stamps displayed was to be the sole or even the most important criterion by which entries were judged, the medals were probably always going to go to the rich. This was unacceptable to the usually very friendly community of collectors and the rules for exhibitions were written so that whilst scarce material was accepted as important the method of presentation of all the material was to be of special importance. The judges are always interested to see material of modest catalogue value which they know in fact to be very difficult to find and they welcome any display which has something new to say or which presents well known material in a new way.

When Jonathan Swift wrote in 1720 'A Letter to a young Clergyman lately entered into Holy Orders' he defined style as 'Proper words in proper places' and went on to say that 'When a man's thoughts are clear, the properest words will generally offer themselves first.' 'Proper material in proper places' might well define the good exhibit if 'Proper words in proper places' have been used to describe it.

The careful reading of the rules, particularly those for competitions and examinations, is always important but even more helpful may be an understanding of the philosophy or logic behind the rules and their interpretation.

I hope to have demonstrated in this chapter that there is nothing special or out of the way about the preparation of an exhibit. The standards by which an article or a short story are judged or a broadcast talk apply equally to a philatelic exhibit. There is a message or story; there is a method of conveying it. In both method and story clarity, skill, novelty and brevity are qualities to be looked for.

The F.I.P.

In June 1926, there was formed in Paris a non-profitmaking association called the *Fédération Internationale de Philatélie*. The F.I.P. is a kind of international watchdog with the task of trying to keep stamp collecting free from a number of practices which might endanger the hobby. We are concerned with the F.I.P. because one of their tasks has been to lay down rules for international philatelic exhibitions held under their sponsorship. Not all international exhibitions of importance are sponsored by the F.I.P. but the majority of them are and most of the rules determined by the F.I.P. are followed in important exhibitions whether the Federation sponsors them or not. It is a general rule that only exhibitors who have obtained a silver medal in a national exhibition or who can provide evidence of being of that standard can submit entries to an international exhibition. There is therefore a general interest in ensuring that all exhibits given a silver medal are of equivalent and adequate quality. It is therefore convenient that national exhibitions should generally conform to the F.I.P's rules and many other exhibitions keep in step with these. Some of the F.I.P's rules are therefore likely to concern the prospective exhibitor even if he does not envisage the final objective of showing internationally.

The F.I.P's rules which concern us here are of two kinds, those which apply to all exhibits and those drawn up especially to regulate exhibits in particular sections e.g. aerophilately or postal history.

The general rules include the provision that the entry must be entirely the property of the exhibitor; that the display of stamps or vignettes be avoided if they have been characterised as undesirable issues by the F.I.P.; that no indication of the monetary value of a piece is allowed.

The object of the first of the rules just mentioned is to prevent 'the unfair competition' which would be provided if a group of collectors combined the finest pieces in their separate collections and exhibited them under one name. The result might be interesting, but it would be rather daunting for other entrants using only their own resources.

The issue by the F.I.P. of directives on undesirable issues is a laudable attempt to restrict and discourage the issue of officially created varieties with the sole intention of getting money out of collectors. These include imperforate versions of stamps normally issued perforated and very limited special issues which are never put on sale for use on mail by the general public. It is sometimes difficult to discover whether a stamp has been banned by the F.I.P. and it must be admitted that time washes away a number of sins, so that many stamps issued earlier in this century at elevated premiums are accepted almost as classics, though had they been issued more recently, they would have been banned.

The rule against the indication of monetary value confirms what is a simple principle of good taste or good manners. It conflicts however with the legitimate interests of the learner or of a specialist in a different field who will like to have his attention drawn to items of special interest. To the uninformed eye all stamps may look very much the same. Discreet reference is therefore allowed to rarity. It may simply take the form of the number issued. On the other hand an explanation that a particular hand-stamp, say, was only in use for an hour or two may do all that is necessary. Schoolboys are discouraged from boasting about their athletic prowess, but they are allowed to wear the bright blazers and 'colours' which make that prowess clear enough. There are ways of writing-up which bring out the scarcity and importance of an exhibitor's favourite possessions without any mention of money.

The general rules of the F.I.P. also provide that if reference is made to the expertisation of an item by an expert or an expert committee the certificate must be available for the jury to see. Some exhibition rules are stricter and determine that no reference to expertisation should appear on the face of an exhibit, though certificates should be at the disposal of the jury.

The majority of the rules laid down by the F.I.P. are best discussed under the heading of the types of exhibition to which they refer: 'Thematic Rules', 'Rules for Aerophilately' etc. But two general rules should be mentioned because they determine whether the exhibit is acceptable for exhibition internationally. They are that exhibitor should belong to an F.I.P. member organisation and that he should have been awarded at least a silver medal in a national exhibition. Most collectors who aspire to be exhibitors will belong to some society affiliated to a national organisation and if they do not they should hasten to join one, if only to get greater enjoyment out of their hobby. The silver medal rule can be waived if 'the competent national federation' is willing to certify that the collection is of silver medal standard. The conditions of entry are rather stricter for stamp dealers who must get a formal certificate from the national federation that the exhibit is a private collection formed by the dealer over a period longer than the last five years.

The Competitive Classes and the Criteria for National and General Classes

In all national and international exhibitions and in major exhibitions at other levels the exhibits are divided into classes so that, to a certain extent, like is judged against like. It is usually quite clear into which class an exhibit belongs, but some may be marginal, so the regulations of all exhibitions allow the organisers to move an exhibit from the class in which it has been submitted to another one which they consider more suitable. This may influence the marking. Slightly different standards, for example, differentiate the general class from the postal history class, so a move from one to the other may be to the advantage of the exhibitor.

In the Amphilex 1977 international exhibition, for example, there were ten competitive classes.

1. Collections of the host country
2. Collections of the colonies of the host country
3. Europe
4. Countries outside Europe
5. Postal history and pre-philately
6. Thematic and Subject collections
7. Air mail
8a. Postal Stationery
8b. Collections not covered by 1-7
9. Junior collections
10. Literature

It was made clear that relevant pre-philatelic and postal stationery items could be included in classes 1-4, but that if these predominated the collections should be submitted in other appropriate classes.

The arrangements for the British Philatelic Exhibition of the same year were similar. Here there were seven competitive classes. A single Class 2 replaced Classes 2, 3, 4, 8a and 8b. This single class was subdivided into (a) postage stamps of Commonwealth countries, (b) postage stamps of foreign countries, and (c) items which do not fall into any other class or into 2a or 2b. A 'cinderella' collection of German local stamps would presumably fall internationally into Class 3 and nationally into Class 2b. A general collection of local stamps would presumably fall into Class 8b internationally and into Class 2c nationally. In cases of doubt the exhibitor should always consult the organisers or their local representative in advance, so that the exhibit can be

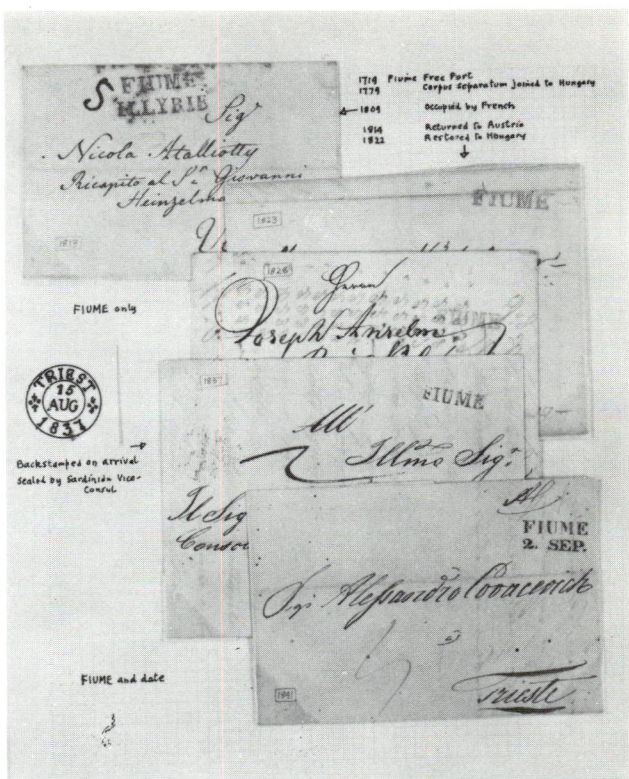

A large number of sheets with just one cover per page can be boring, and judicious overlapping can help. Care must be taken to ensure that the overlapping does not obscure important postal markings. These covers are shown in date sequence, providing information with economy.

prepared in the way which will best bring out its virtues in the context of the agreed class.

International exhibitions vary a little from one to another. For instance Internaba 1974 held in Basle understandably did not have a class devoted to the host's colonial possessions. It did however have a class devoted to 'Collections based on special ideas'. This was in addition to one for thematic collections.

The F.I.P. lays down the criteria by which the exhibits in the general classes should be judged. These are:

1. The philatelic knowledge and personal research of which the exhibit gives evidence.
2. The standard reached by the exhibit.
3. The rarity and the condition of the items.
4. The quality of the presentation.

The Federation does not however determine the exact weight to be given to each of the four criteria. It is however perhaps legitimate to assume that they are quoted in the rules in their order of importance. If this is so, we may suppose that an advanced collection which shows evidence of philatelic knowledge and research (Criteria 2 and 1) will take precedence over one which is merely outstanding for the rarity and condition of the pieces shown and the quality of the presentation. In fact for the higher medals an exhibit must be noteworthy under all the four headings.

The organisers of the British national exhibitions help entrants by advising them of the way in which the jury have been instructed to divide the marks they allot between the different criteria.

	A	B
Philatelic knowledge, personal research and personal study	30	30
Importance of the exhibit	30	
Importance and special factors		20
Rarity		10
Presentation	20	20
Condition	20	20
	100	100

It will be seen that in exhibition A no particular mention of rarity is made and that even in exhibition B it is only given 10% of the total marks. Some account of rarity is however taken under the heading of importance, a heading which will be discussed in more detail later. The important difference between rarity and high catalogue value has already been emphasised. Even beginners soon discover that many stamps of high catalogue value are regularly offered by dealers and at auctions; the collector with enough money can get them almost by return of post. On the other hand some cheaper stamps, even those priced in the catalogues in pence, are very difficult to find. Since the juries try to acknowledge achievement rather than a long purse, it is to this kind of rarity that they pay particular attention.

This is, however, only part of the story. The jury are also concerned to determine the standard reached by the exhibit and must pay attention to the degree of completeness which the collector has achieved. In some subjects for collection the stamps of high catalogue value are so important that their absence is at once noticeable. The collector has to resign himself to this and if his means do not allow him to approach completeness he should be prepared to accept that this subject is not a suitable one for him, if he is interested in exhibiting. It saves disappointment later if a careful survey is made of likely commitments before a decision is taken to specialise.

As is being constantly emphasised throughout this guide there are only a few absolute rules and many of the decisions which distinguish a good exhibit from a bad one are matters of taste and judgment. It is not possible to affirm that failure to obtain, say, the top five most costly stamps is acceptable, but not failure to obtain some of the next five or ten in order of cost. The inclusion of a stamp in the catalogue does not mean that it is essential. The belief that it is leads, particularly on the Continent, to ridiculous discussions. The Italian 1,000 Lire parcel post stamp was first issued in 1954 with the then current winged wheel watermark. Two and a half years later the same value was printed on paper with the multiple star watermark. Many collectors ignored the original issue until its catalogue value had risen. It stands now, as I write, at nearly £500. Some of the collectors who did not obtain this stamp when it was first issued campaigned to get the star watermarked version accepted by the catalogues as the normal issue and the winged wheel one as a variety with an 'a' number. This would have enabled them to claim that they were complete 'except for varieties'.

The results of the break up of the Austro-Hungarian Empire at the end of the first world war can be made the subject of a very interesting collection which, in my judgment, would in no way be marred by the absence of the overprinted high value stamps catalogued at over £1,000 and often never properly sold at post offices, but distributed as a favour to officials. These stamps can be rejected for reasons very acceptable to the connoisseur. Sometimes the collector will have to admit that his exhibit would be much improved if only his purse permitted. Even in these cases skilful arrangement of the material will lessen the impact of the gaps and may even disguise their presence. Obvious gaps are acceptable in a reference collection; in an exhibit they invite an unfavourable verdict.

On condition it is possible to be more dogmatic. It is the characteristic of the connoisseur in almost every field that he gives great attention to the quality of the pieces in his collection. Since a few bad copies can destroy the visual impact of an exhibit their inclusion can only be justified if there are very special reasons, the most satisfactory of which is the fact that good copies do not exist. It is better to leave out a stamp rather than risk spoiling the effect. If a stamp has been repaired and this is not indicated, the jury has the right to downgrade the exhibit for this reason alone. The condition of wreck covers is an exception. It is of their nature not to be pristine. Logically it is only to genuine pieces that the rules about condition should apply, but the importance of condition is so firmly established in the minds of collectors and jurymen that I have, for instance, been criticised for including, by the way of reference and with clear indication of their nature, forgeries which were not perfect specimens!

For some collectors, particularly on the Continent, a modern stamp with the trace of a hinge on the back is imperfect. This is a matter of controversy and will be discussed in a later chapter.

The Material and its Presentation

The chapters of this guide so far have been devoted to arguing the importance of choosing a new or interesting theme and to demonstrating it in a logical way. The theme should be illustrated where possible by carefully selected philatelic material rather than by words, and in both illustration and description there is an obligation to be concise. Two covers with the same features are nearly as bad as two sentences saying the same thing. The ability to develop a theme logically, concisely and with a certain elegance of expression is regarded as a quality in very many fields. It is the result of a mixture of talent, education and experience. A guide or handbook cannot do more than give hints. So it is time to turn now from the logical development of the theme to its presentation on the album pages.

Some of the discussion on presentation which follows may appear elementary. Some elementary advice is purposely included because the opinion of one judge 'presentation of the exhibit seems to receive scant attention by some entrants' will be echoed by many others who have served on juries. Even in serious exhibitions most judges can remember exhibits on grubby album pages scarred by fingermarks and by hinge marks where unwanted stamps have been removed, exhibits in which damaged stamps disfigured by heavy postmarks were mounted crookedly and

out of line and crowded so close to each other that even the good specimens could not be properly enjoyed.

The collector who is asked to provide an exhibit of 32 sheets will often be tempted simply to remove 32 pages from his album and send them along. This will rarely work well, though the experienced exhibitor will often be able to arrange the layout of the pages in his collection so that a certain number of them can be used in different sequences as part of an exhibit.

Quality of the Material

The exhibitor's first task is to check the quality of the material. Some may have to be rejected because the stamp is torn or cut into, has damaged perforations, is thinned, creased, or spoiled by unsightly stains or heavy postmarking. A stamp is thinned when part of the back of the paper has been removed by careless removal from the envelope or album page or because the gum has become moist and has stuck it to the album page. The thinning may not be visible from the front, but if the jury, who have the right to observe the quality of individual stamps, are aware of it they will certainly mark the exhibit down.

'Beautification' of stamps to conceal tears and other fundamental operations of this sort are not permitted, but some simple cosmetic treatment is allowed. For instance used stamps may be much improved by a simple wash in cool water, but when wet they should be handled very carefully. Stamps or covers spotted with brown or yellow stains should not be allowed in a collection let alone an exhibit, not only because they are unsightly, but also because the stain is usually caused by a fungus which in time destroys the paper and which spreads easily from stamp to album page and is often airborne to other stamps nearby. If the damage is not far advanced very careful application of a ten per cent solution of Chloramine-T on the tip of a paint brush may both check and remove the stain. Used stamps can be inserted in the solution provided that they tolerate water. (A few colours are sensitive to this treatment so if the stamp or cover is valuable take advice first.) Envelopes in a collection can be treated more radically and tears should be carefully closed. One of the best ways of doing this is to apply a small quantity of good quality paste to the back of the paper behind the tear and press on a little piece of tissue paper so that the tear will be kept

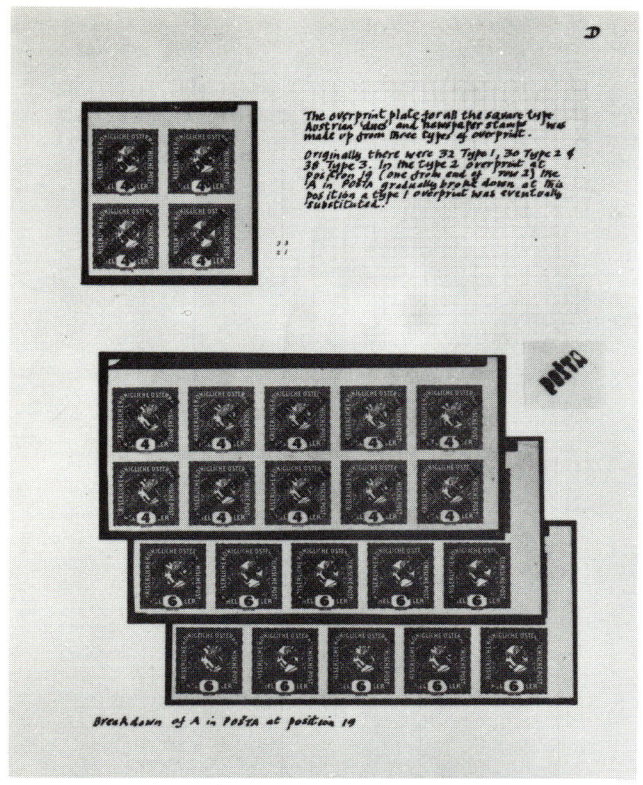

The overprint plate for all the square type Austrian 'ducs' and newspaper stamps was made up from three types of overprint.

Originally there were 32 Type 1, 30 Type 2 & 38 Type 3. In the Type 2 overprint at position 19 (one from end of row 2) the 'A' in POSTA gradually broke down at this position a type 1 overprint was eventually substituted.

Breakdown of A in POSTA at position 19

Here attention is being drawn to a constant variety in one stamp in the lower row of each block. If the blocks had not been overlapped they would have had to be broken up or placed on separate pages, making comparison more difficult.

closed and the paper not noticeably thickened. Before being inserted in the exhibit light envelopes should be stiffened by inserting a thin white card carefully cut to size. Dirty envelopes can be cleaned by the careful application of breadcrumbs or an artist's eraser-cleaner, all rubbing being outwards from the centre to the edges, otherwise there is danger of creasing. Practice on an ordinary envelope may help prevent a serious disaster later on through lack of skill.

Used stamps can be mounted in the collection 'on piece', that is with enough of the surrounding envelope or card for the postmark to be seen as well as the stamp. All four sides of the piece should be straight. In my judgment it does not matter if they form a perfect rectangle, the occasional variation from the rectangle may help avoid monotony, but it is important that no attempt is made to form a fancy shape, even of the simplest kind. In an interesting collection which I bought some time ago all the pieces had been given rounded corners. This attracted attention away from the stamp to the paper surrounding it and would be found distasteful by most judges. If the stamp is floated off the piece before mounting, which it usually is, the operation must be complete and it is best that no gum is left on the back. It is very important that all the perforation holes are clear. A used stamp with little pieces of paper still adhering to part of the outline is not acceptable. Creases in used stamps and covers should, if possible, be ironed out.

Mounting

Juries often complain of the poor way in which stamps are mounted onto the page, either because they are crooked or out of alignment or because they are not properly fixed to the page and fall off. These irregularities so spoil the appearance of the pages that many British judges recommend the use of stamp hinges for both unused and used stamps. Modern hinges if properly used leave only the slightest trace and should fix the material safely to the album page. The newcomer to collecting, however, should be reminded that the market value of stamps which are unmounted mint may be considerably higher than that for mounted mint; this is particularly true on the Continent. This is not the place to discuss whether this is sensible, but it is right to warn the collector that sometimes when he affixes a hinge to a previously unmounted stamp he may be halving its resale value, or even reducing it by two thirds. If this is unacceptable to the exhibitor he will have to use the 'strip' type of mount, the most popular being known as *Hawid* mounts. In these mounts the stamp is held between two plastic layers. The back of one of the layers is coated with adhesive and this layer not the stamp is stuck to the page. It is convenient to talk of 'strips' since in the beginning these items of philatelic stationery were always sold in this form, to be cut down to the appropriate width by the collector. It is now possible to get them already cut to size, which can be very helpful if the country collected only uses a limited number of sizes in stamps.

The disadvantages of strips are that stamps do move around a little in them and can fall out and that the transparent plastic does seem to remove a little of the bloom from the front of a mint stamp in some instances. Their use may also be a little time-consuming, especially if they have to be cut to size. The background of most strips is black and it is very important that this black border is narrow. If the strips are cut too wide the border will be considered funereal. There is a slight danger that when the back of the strip is moistened by the tongue a little moisture may overlap the edge and get between the stamp-retaining layers where it will spread. If this happens the stamp may get moist. However the plastic surface usually rejects ordinary gum and if the strip is allowed to dry out the stamp can be later removed very little damaged. To diminish the risk of this danger it is my practice not to use the adhesive on the back to fix strips to album pages, but to do so with a stamp hinge.

The advantage of strips is primarily that the use of hinges on the back of mint stamps is avoided. There are possibly two other advantages. Because rust mold does not seem to multiply on plastic, stamps in strips seem to be less prone to rust (foxing). The other advantage can be a substantial one for the keen exhibitor who may sometimes wish to use one and the same group of stamps to illustrate two themes, e.g. designers and postal rates. Album sheets are prepared with only the appropriate strips on them but otherwise complete writing-up. Then, immediately before exhibition, all that is necessary is to insert the right stamps into the waiting, empty strips.

A modified form of strip is now marketed under the name *Showgard* which instead of leaving three sides open leaves only two. This does inhibit unwanted movement of stamps but has the disadvantage that strips can only be cut to size horizontally which means that a greater stock of sizes must be kept and it is not quite so easy to ensure the correct narrow margins of black round the stamp. However, because the strips of this type hold the stamp firmly it is possible to mount them sideways so that only one size of strip is needed for landscape and portrait format stamps, provided that the dimensions of both are the same. If the *Hawid* strips are mounted on their side there is danger that stamps will fall out quite easily.

Postcards and covers in ordinary collections should not be hinged to the page. This either stains the back of the cover or leaves a small cleaner area which contrasts with the rest. It is best to use transparent photo-corners or their equivalent made for collectors.

Some collectors like to use a background of paper or thin card to isolate a card, cover or stamp from the grille of the album page. The background may be white, black or a neutral colour such as grey. If used, backgrounds should be modest in size and colour, otherwise the eye is attracted to the background away from the stamp or cover. I do not myself believe that these backgrounds help the presentation of cards or covers, but I think that there is a strong argument for using carefully cut mats for both used and unused stamps.

If the stamp is mounted on the mat and the mat in its turn mounted in the album, the assembly can be moved without touching the stamp. The mat may have to be rehinged, but not the stamp. This is a method of obtaining some of the advantages of hinging without its disadvantages. Although preservation of the stamp is probably the strongest argument in favour of mats, the visual separation between the stamp and the page which they supply can increase the quality of the presentation which can be given added variety if, say, black mats are used for unused stamps, white mats for used stamps, and grey mats for forgeries shown for reference. The use of mats increases the thickness of the album, so some kind of guard should be used at the binding side of the page so that the thickness at either edge

Photocopying allows marks on the back of a cover to be displayed without splitting the cover open or having to use a second cover to show the marks. Some judges would object to the photograph of a seaplane base here, but it does not diminish the impact of the cover, adds variety to the arrangement and provides interest for the non-specialist.

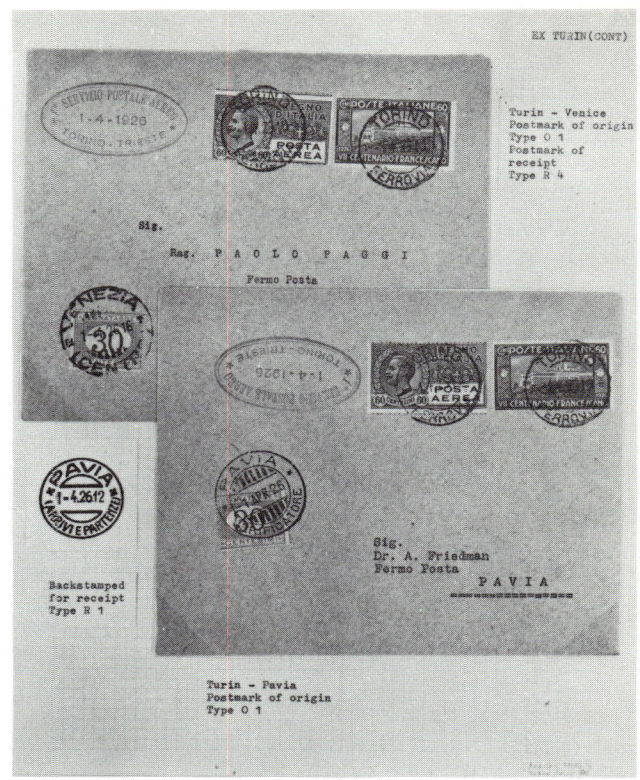

Turin - Venice
Postmark of origin
Type O 1
Postmark of
receipt
Type R 4

Sig.
Rag. P A O L O P A G G I
Fermo Posta

Sig.
Dr. A. Friedman
Fermo Posta
P A V I A

Backstamped
for receipt
Type R 1

Turin - Pavia
Postmark of origin
Type O 1

A very economical text is possible on this page as references are carried forward from the previous one (illustrated on page 13).

of the album is about equal. If coloured mats are used, the colours chosen should be muted and the paper should be tested to ensure that the colour is not liable to come off on the back of the stamp, and damage it.

Stamps arranged on a page form a pattern which can be varied a little according to the taste of the collector. Aesthetic arguments are not the only valid ones; some layouts are more logical than others. The collector has a choice, the elements of which are the number of stamps in a line, the distance between lines, the number of lines to a page and the distance between stamps. There are certain generally agreed aesthetic rules which are best not broken unless there is some special justification. They are that: the page should not appear either too empty or too full; the layout should be simple and fancy patterns, e.g. triangles or letter formations, are judged to detract from the stamps; if possible without affectation there should be variety in the arrangement of successive pages; the presentation of stamps in sequence of face value is not essential, particularly where the stamps of a series are in two or three differing shapes (it is usually best to group the shapes). There is difference of opinion as to the best ordering of a series of nine stamps. Three rows each of three would probably

14

be rejected because the stamps looked too far apart, but there would be no general agreement as to the best between 1-4-4, 2-4-3 or 4-4-1. If the size of sheet and space allowed, 4-5 or 5-4 would be preferred to any of the earlier three.

Whatever decision is taken about the number of lines and stamps in the lines, it is important that stamps which belong to a series should be displayed in a way which makes this clear. It is wrong to display two series each of eight stamps in four rows of four, each row being separated by an equal distance from the row above. There should be a wider gap between the second and third row to mark the separate series.

It is sometimes said that not more than one cover should appear on a page. This may be a good general rule but it seems to me to be no more than that. One cover per page throughout a display can be very monotonous, so possibilities of varying the layout should be welcomed. If all the markings of interest happen to be on the right-hand side of an envelope it may be possible to mount two other envelopes above the first envelope so that the second and third envelopes eclipse the envelope below, leaving only the right-hand side visible. This is a useful method where similar postal markings have to be compared since it brings three types of marking into close proximity.

If more than two covers are mounted on a page one or other of them can, if necessary, be allowed to extend over the edge of the printed (grille) surface of the page. Only in very exceptional circumstances should *stamps* be placed outside the printed area.

It is a matter of experience for an exhibitor to develop alternative layouts and the best ways of achieving an effect which has the freshness of reasonable variety in appealing to the eye and which also emphasises visually the logic of the writing-up.

Writing-up

The logical development of a theme can be much helped by the way in which the material is laid out. If the material is carefully grouped and arranged, the eye will follow the sequence and understand. It is unlikely however that the theme can be properly put over by the layout of the material alone, so there must usually be some writing-up. The writing-up should be brief, it should concentrate on what is important and it should be closely associated with the material displayed. If it is all these things it will help bring the whole exhibit into focus.

The physical part of writing-up worries many exhibitors who are self-conscious about their handwriting. Some of them decide to get the work done by an expert penman. The necessity and the desirability of doing this must be a matter of opinion and vary from person to person. I believe that a collection should reflect the personality of the collector and happily accept a little irregularity in the penmanship. I also believe that most people can write legibly if they write slowly.

Some people hold strong views about writing-up; they consider that it should all be in ink, that a typewriter should not be used, that a mixture of typing and writing is not acceptable. If a member of a jury does hold these opinions strongly there is a possibility that it may influence his judgment against a collection, but I am sure only marginally. My own views are of a piece, I hope, with the rest of my attitude to the presentation of stamps. I believe them to be logical. The writing up is part of the process of communication. It should therefore be legible and if possible should allow differences in emphasis to be marked. If it also conveys some of the personality of the collector, that is all the better. If it is in handwriting it should be in ink, the ink should be black or dark blue, and waterproof. Brightly coloured inks and fancy lettering should be avoided, because they draw attention away from the stamps. Waterproof ink is safer, because, if the page is accidently wetted, it will not run and damage the stamps.

Emphasis can be provided by the use of capitals, underlining and possibly the use of slightly larger upper and lower case letters. But the emphasis must be used sparingly, otherwise it becomes not emphasis but just one long shout. The underlining of the whole manuscript text serves only to make it more difficult to read as does writing the whole text in capitals. Why do people mistakenly believe that it is easier to write legible capitals than legible small letters? What educated person would find reading a whole novel all set in capitals tolerable?

It is generally agreed that the frames which contain an exhibit should show some unity in presentation. If, for example, mounting stamps on mats appeals to the collector, all the stamps should be so mounted. Just as it is unsatisfactory to move from a page with all the stamps on mats to one with all the stamps mounted directly onto the page, it is disturbing to move from pages all written up in ink to those all typewritten. However it is quite acceptable to my judgment that the main lines of the writing up should be type-written whilst short notes alongside the stamps are handwritten. The different styles provide appropriately different emphasis.

If the writing-up is to be typewritten it is best not done directly onto the album page where the type will be confused by the lines of the grid but onto white or off-white paper of about the same shade as the album page. The paper panels containing the text are carefully cut out and pasted to the album page. It is usually unnecessary to paste the whole strip; it is best just to apply a small dab of adhesive at either end. Before the strip is pasted down it should be moved about the page to discover the best position. It is often possible to balance an unbalanced short set of stamps with the panel of writing-up. A series of two stamps, for example, can be hinged in toward the left margin and the text fixed at the same level toward the right margin. Typing onto panels rather than the page not only enables the best position to be checked, it also enables mistakes to be corrected without having to destroy an album page. All that has to be destroyed is the small panel on which the text was typed. It is my personal opinion that these information panels are best placed below the series or cover they describe, not above them.

Those who have not used a typewriter for writing up may not realise that it is not as inflexible a medium as may at first appear. Emphasis can be given by the use of capitals or by underlining. A little experimentation will demonstrate the flexibility of typescript. Here there is space only for these general indications. The use of red typescript for emphasis is usually disliked as is surrounding the information panels with a black frame line. I can however see no objection to very small titles being neatly framed in black.

The collector who is not a skilled draftsman will find illustrative drawings a great problem. If they are badly done they stand out aggressively from the page. Bad draftsmen are wise therefore to include as few as possible. Though it may be necessary to show a drawing of a postmark which is out of sight on the back of a cover, it is rarely ever necessary to draw one which is visible on the front. The problem may sometimes be circumvented by making a photostat copy of the concealed postmark and, cutting it out neatly, fixing it to the page in the way other information panels are. If the mark is traced onto tracing paper it can be given an opaque look if pasted first to a square of white paper before being pasted onto the album page. Tracing paper

drawings pasted directly onto the album page let the grid show through disturbingly. Enlarged photographs of detail to be illustrated can also help. Sometimes they can be pasted onto the album page, but it is probably better to use them as an aid to drawing. A thin sheet of white paper is placed over the photograph and a strong light is projected through the back of the photograph enabling the detail to be traced onto the paper. The paper with tracing is subsequently pasted into the album. Sometimes the detail in the photograph is not clear enough for tracing through paper. It may have to be inked in on the photograph for greater clarity. There is a method of bleaching away the part of the photograph not inked in, which will make the detail clearer. All these are general matters of writing-up and not solely of exhibitions, so need not be discussed further.

When we study the schedule of marks allotted in the British national exhibitions we find that fifty per cent of the marks in one instance and sixty per cent in the other is allotted to a combination of factors described as philatelic knowledge, personal research or study, and importance. The term personal research is liable to be misunderstood. As is made clear in the accompanying literature the organisers intend it to mean study of the published information and not necessarily original work done by the exhibitor for which he will be given credit 'under the heading of importance'.

For half the marks they give, we can conclude, the jury look for evidence in the writing-up and in the layout of the exhibit that the entrant has read carefully the published literature on his specialisation. This it may not be easy to do. The selection of serious books on stamp collecting in public libraries is not very great. It may be just adequate for the well trodden fields such as Great Britain, but very few libraries have works on foreign countries. Some local philatelic societies have libraries as do most specialist societies. The National Philatelic Society has a good library and the Royal Philatelic Society, London, an outstanding one. From all of these, books may be borrowed by members. Local libraries are pleased to try and get for enquirers books which are absent from their shelves but perhaps available in other libraries. The largest public philatelic library on the Continent is that belonging to the Munich City Library (Stadtbibliothek München, Philatelistische Bibliothek, D-8000 München 5, Pestalozzistrasse 2, W. Germany) and the largest public philatelic library in the United States

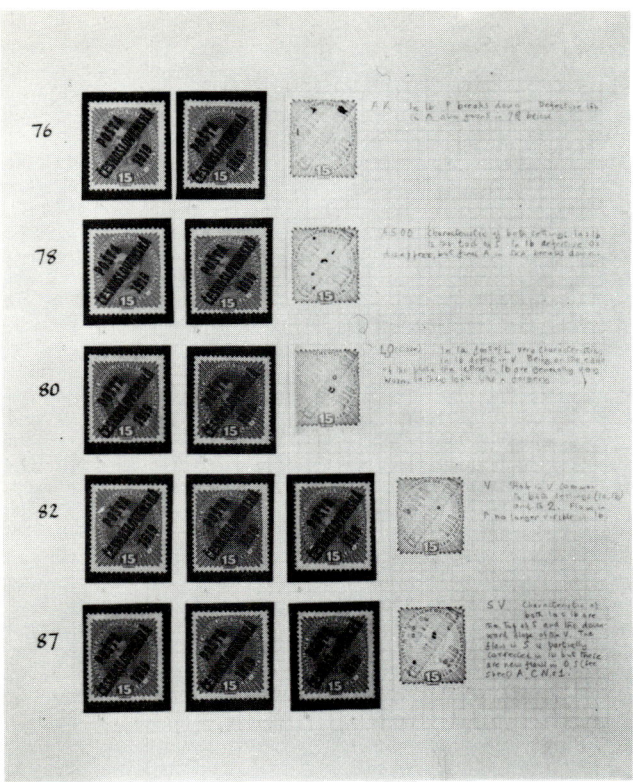

At specialist exhibitions artistic layout can rightly be sacrificed in favour of succinct communication of information. In this plating study the arrangement is strictly practical. The light photocopies to show the varieties do not compete with the stamps. Writing-up is in pencil as the study is tentative.

is that of the American Philatelic Research Library (P.O. Box 338 State College, Pennsylvania, U.S.A.). Regulations change from time to time, but both of the libraries last mentioned will probably be willing to provide for a fee photocopies of significant articles in otherwise unobtainable journals. Last but not least there is always the possibility of buying the necessary literature! If this is done at the time of publication the purchase price will usually be amply repaid by the information obtained. It is however a characteristic weakness of a large number of collectors that they are pleased to spend much money on the current fashionable triviality and spend very little on literature. The result of this is that philatelic books for specialists are usually published in small editions and when these at last run out the books can only be obtained, if at all, at high prices at auction. It may be a consolation to the exhibitor who only discovers the appropriate literature after long search that the length of the search probably means that the information is not generally known. This will usually make his search of unclassified material more rewarding and it will often mean that the pages of his exhibit will give information not known to visitors to the exhibition and perhaps not to the jury either. This will make it more interesting and worth more marks.

If the exhibitor who reads twice as much about his stamps as other entrants simply fills his pages with twice as much information, nothing will be achieved. His objective is similar to that of the social historian. He reads widely, first to discover the facts and secondly to distinguish those of importance from the rest. Curiously a number of collectors whose working hours demand the kind of selective judgment mentioned abandon it altogether in the leisure time they devote to collecting. Many good exhibits are spoiled because the importance of selection and correct emphasis is not understood, so it may be helpful to give some examples.

Almost all the stamps of Great Britain issued from 1934 onwards have been printed in photogravure by Harrison and Sons Ltd. and comb perforated 15 x 14. It is therefore quite unnecessary to indicate these facts alongside every series; particulars of perforation or printing should only be mentioned where they are exceptional. This will help give emphasis to the exceptions and will allow space for other information to be written in, such as the name of the designer, if the collector is interested in this important part of stamp production or, perhaps, occasional explanation of the change in face value reflecting the change in rates now more common in inflationary times. What is not necessary, as one sometimes sees, is the entry of the catalogue number beneath each stamp. This makes no contribution to the intelligent 'reading' of the page; it takes up space better used otherwise for important information or for blank space to set off the stamp; it is a habit universally disliked by juries.

There are occasions when, in order to distinguish two apparently similar stamps of, say, the same value, it is helpful to note the different catalogue numbers. But even here it is prudent to show as well the dates of issue or other identifying information because catalogue numbers can change and the reference may cease to be accurate. Where it is known at the time of writing that there is a possibility of a change of number or a revision of information it is my practice to use pencil for the writing-up so that

alterations can be made later without destroying the page. Some judges are so tied to uniformity in the writing-up that they object to this; I believe that it is sensible and has the added advantage of indicating different levels of certainty in the information conveyed.

Everyone is agreed that if possible the material should be left to tell its own tale. This is easy enough where ordinary issues of stamps are concerned; it is more difficult for varieties, errors and, particularly, stamps on cover. Most intelligent collectors like to know why a variety occurred, not only out of general interest but also because they know that certain kinds of variety can only have occurred with the deliberate connivance of the printer, which makes them of less perhaps of no interest to the collector. On an envelope there is so much which may be of interest—accountancy marks, transit marks, curious routes or uses etc. There may also be important markings on the back.

Juries, we are told, have no time for reading They only want to look at material. Even if this is true of juries it may not be true of visitors to an exhibition, so the collector has a double responsibility, to the visitor and to the jury. He must decide by exercising craftsman's judgement But if experience in other fields counts here too it is not length which discourages reading but a boring and unreadable style. Novel and interesting information is quickly absorbed. Too much condensation may make matter difficult to read not quicker. Remember that the same judge who blames an entrant for writing too much may mark him down later for not drawing attention to something of significance. Wrong or inaccurate information can make a very damaging impression.

Throughout the discussion the word 'significance' keeps recurring and each time it recurs it begs the question, since one man's significance may be another man's poison. Fortunately there is, among those with more than a year or two of collecting experience, some measure of agreement. Whether he admits to it or not the modern serious collector is always a postal historian in the sense that he collects items associated with the social history of the postal services. He may limit his interest to a single aspect of that history, such as the labels used to prepay postage, or the wide field of the postal markings on a letter which reflect changes in postal administration, the vicissitudes of war, and many of the influences which, because they affect the lives of human beings also affect their means of communicating

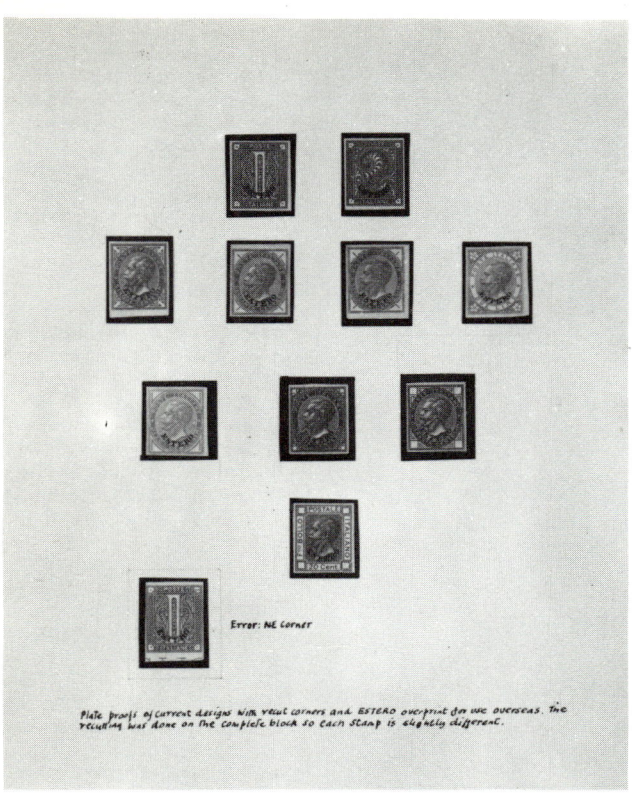

Error: NE Corner

Plate proofs of current designs with rent corners and ESTERO overprint for use overseas. The retouching was done on the complete block so each stamp is slightly different.

On this page all the stamps in the third row had margins. They have been covered with black paper, over which is hinged a panel of paper cut from a similar album page. At a distance this is scarcely noticeable, but see the enlarged illustration below.

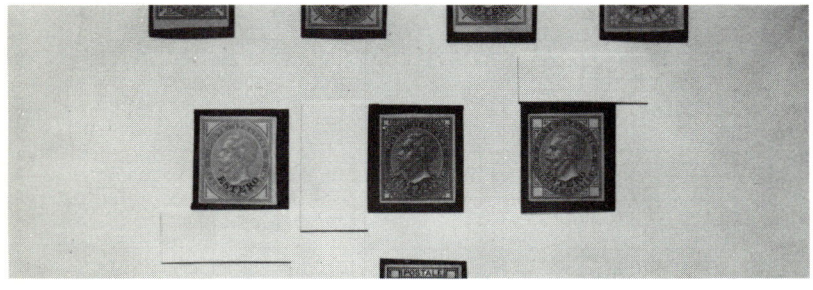

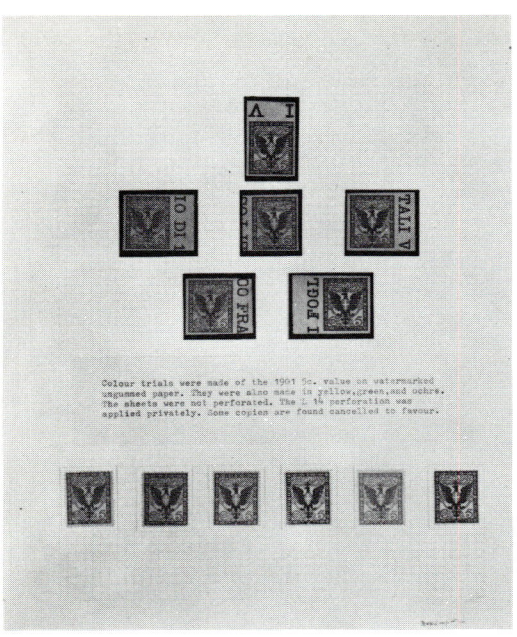

Colour trials were made of the 1901 5c. value on watermarked ungummed paper. They were also made in yellow,green,and ochre. The sheets were not perforated. The L 1½ perforation was applied privately. Some copies are found cancelled to favour.

Sheet margins can interfere with the balance of the display, but cutting them off can destroy vital positional evidence or diminish the value of the stamp. Here a little imagination has been used to make the margins balance.

with each other. Changes in postal markings due to wars are likely to be considered more important than those due to the carelessness of postal clerks in, say, inserting the calendar upside down in the date stamp. Social historians are not only interested in human beings and organisations, they also have concern for the machines they use and their development. So interest in the printing and perforation of stamps is understandable. This interest is pursued in great detail. Many hours are sometimes spent in identifying the particular printed characteristics of each stamp in a sheet. In earlier printing of stamps, particularly in lithography and in recess printing, this detailed study does enable the student to work out very often how the printing plate was built up. It is also often invaluable in helping the identification of dangerous forgeries. It must be admitted,

however, that some of the plating done cannot be logically evaluated; it simply reflects the pleasure many connoisseurs derive from prolonged study of detail. It is a convention of the hobby which often attaches importance to a tiny detail in a classic stamp and denies it to a similar detail in a modern stamp printed by photogravure. If a jury feels, perhaps wrongly, that a particular study has been easy, they may well underestimate its importance. The confident assertion that 'philatelic trivia can never hope to receive a high award even if accompanied by writing-up of a high order' is a useful warning to the intending exhibitor, but it is no more. Pioneers in new philatelic areas may have to be patient just as modern artists have to be. Some of what seems trivial today may, in time, win great respect.

What I have said of the connection between social history and philately does not apply in the same way to thematic collecting which is the subject of a separate chapter.

Final Remarks
Suggestions for arranging and writing up the general collection have been discussed in some detail, because what applies to the general collection applies to almost all other kinds of collection. This is understandable because the object of exhibits of all kinds is to communicate and communication depends on careful logical arrangement of the material, emphasis of the important, clarity of expression and where possible brevity.

Distractions of all sorts are best avoided. This is why a tidy presentation has more impact than a messy one. This is why unity of presentation is desirable. Album leaves should all be of the same size and colour; the manner of arrangement and writing up should be consistent: different aspects of the theme should be separated. Remember that the pages will not be shown in isolation, but grouped in a frame. The number of sheets that the frames hold will be clearly indicated in the exhibition prospectus; in a national exhibition it is likely to be either nine or sixteen standard sheets. Some exhibitors with a laudable regard for detail take account of this in preparing their exhibit and lay out the sheets as they will appear in the frames, making adjustments to improve the general impact. Since the noble volunteers who fill the frames cannot guess a collector's intention all sheets should be clearly numbered

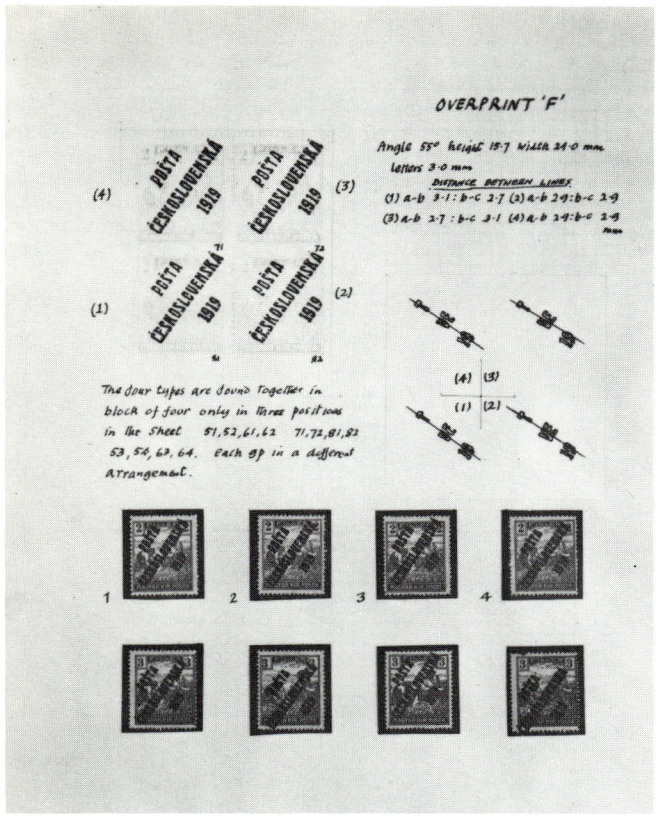

In a specialised exhibit the stamps should always have priority, but in this case the information is vital to the study and space for stamps has had to be sacrificed.

in sequence as indicated in the prospectus. They should be enclosed in transparent protective covers of good quality with the binding edges of album pages and any protective interleaving folded back into the protective cover out of the way.

Because a degree of unity in the presentation is desirable some judges dislike used and unused stamps appearing on the same page. If they are clearly separated this does not worry me, say with the unused series at the top of the page and the used series below. All judges dislike used and unused stamps being mixed in the same series. This sometimes creates problems for the collector. There are many series in which all but one or two stamps can be found unused at reasonable prices. The one or two mentioned however, may be very scarce indeed unused and well out of range of the pocket of the collector. Does he break the rule and include a used specimen to demonstrate the series in its entirety or does he leave a blank? I suggest that he should do neither.

He should lay out the unused series so that the presentation accommodates only those stamps which are, for him, obtainable.

It is an understood and legitimate part of the gamesmanship of exhibitions that the exhibitor need not go out of his way to draw attention to gaps. (This is not so where exhibits are prepared for the information of specialist societies where they are best planned as illustrated handbooks and here the exhibitor should not be ashamed to show his pages 'warts and all'.) If he wishes to show the complete series he should put an indication alongside the series, perhaps an asterisk, or incorporate one in the writing-up. The asterisk will draw the viewer's attention to another part of the page where the one or two used examples will be mounted alongside a text which explains, say, that for such and such reasons the majority of unused examples were destroyed. This procedure can be reversed where the basic collection is of used stamps and one or two unused versions are shown as it were in the

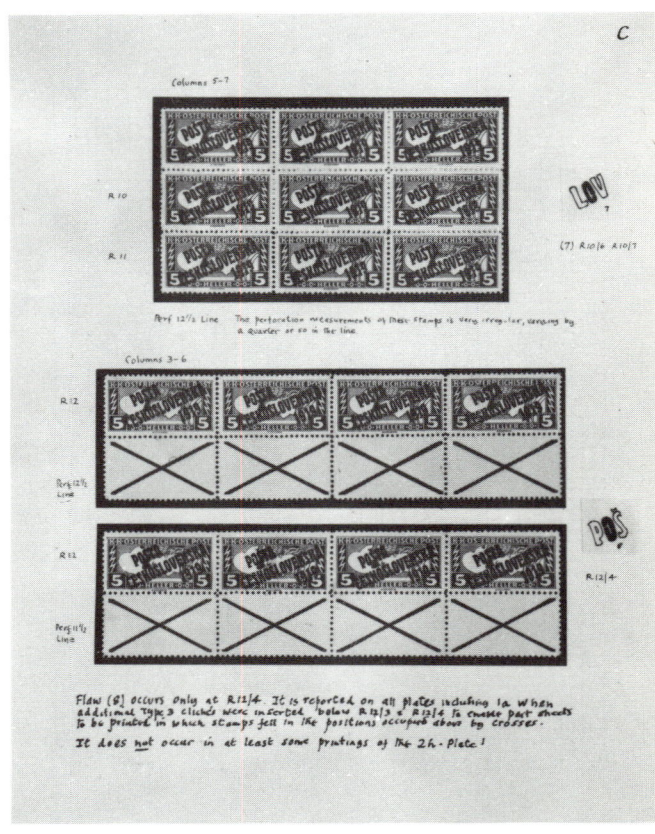

The use of multiples often helps to give the necessary emphasis to the stamps. Note here the use of thick and thin writing-up to convey different emphasis.

margin. Though I use the expression in the margin to indicate that the pieces shown are marginal to the general display, I do not wish to suggest that the stamps should be literally affixed to the margin of the page (this is not a satisfactory position for stamps) but rather that they should be displayed separately on the page. I have explained the method at greater length elsewhere (see 'Footnote Philately' in *Stamp Collecting*, 6 September 1973). Footnotes of this sort are comparable to footnotes in a book; they are ancillary to the main theme.

Since collections are meant to reflect the social history of the communication of information by mail, all material should do this. Exhibits should not reflect the plans and contrivances of dealers to create special material for collectors. Marks will always be given for genuine commercial covers and stamps which appear to have been properly used for prepaying the transport of letters. It is not always possible to distinguish artificial creations from genuine mail and it must be accepted that a great number of early air mail covers were arranged by dealers and did not contain messages of love and affection or commercial orders. Envelope after envelope all to the same addressee create a poor impression and should, if possible, be avoided.

Juries are inclined to be conservative as, I believe, are most stamp collectors. Even though they may pay lip service to studies of recent stamps and out of the way countries, they usually prefer the classics. Those who enjoy the pleasure of treading new pastures must be just a little more careful and a little more persuasive. In the long run it will be worth while. This applies not only to the subject matter of collecting but also to the method of presentation. Interesting pointers can sometimes be obtained by studying the layout of typematter and illustration in periodicals such as *Architectural Review* and *Architectural Journal* which are edited by professionals who are concerned about communication and the visual arts. I believe that a degree of conservatism is desirable, but share Emerson's opinion that 'a foolish consistency is the hobgoblin of little minds'. Provided the exhibitor fixes his attention on the simple objectives outlined in the first paragraph of this chapter, I believe that his display is likely to be effective.

The Postal History Exhibit

Almost everything which has been said about preparing collections for exhibition in the general class applies to postal history exhibits, but there are one or two changes in emphasis which deserve attention.

The F.I.P. have established four headings under which the postal history class is to be judged. These are: (1) treatment of the subject, knowledge of postal history, and research undertaken; (2) importance of the collection and rarities; (3) state of preservation of the collection; (4) presentation. (The French text of the F.I.P. regulation is definitive. I have retranslated and repunctuated the English version which seemed to me to be inaccurate.) The British national exhibitions have grouped these headings similarly and have told exhibitors in the prospectuses how they will be marked.

B1. Knowledge and personal study	40
B2. Originality and importance	25
B3. Relative condition and rarity	15
B4. Presentation, write up and arrangement	20
	100

In one or two matters of detail I find the F.I.P. formulation preferable to the British. In Britain the judges only have to ask (B1), How much does the exhibitor know? How much work has he done? The international rules add an important further question, How has he developed the theme? The British headings associate rarity and condition (B3) which at first sight seems logical, since the rarer the stamp or cover the more tolerant one may be about its condition, but in history the rarity of the documentation must take second place to its importance. In other words the jury should honour the study which illuminates a neglected or misunderstood passage of postal history above an assembly of scarce pieces illustrating an old theme. The F.I.P. headings do not say that they must do this, but by grouping importance and rarity together it enables them to give full marks under the section, if they wish, to a collection which they judge to be important, even if the theme is not illustrated by many rarities.

The discussion in the last paragraph is not hair-splitting. It is fundamental to an understanding of the particular character of the postal history class. It should remind exhibitors that the quality of their history is more important than rarity and presentation.

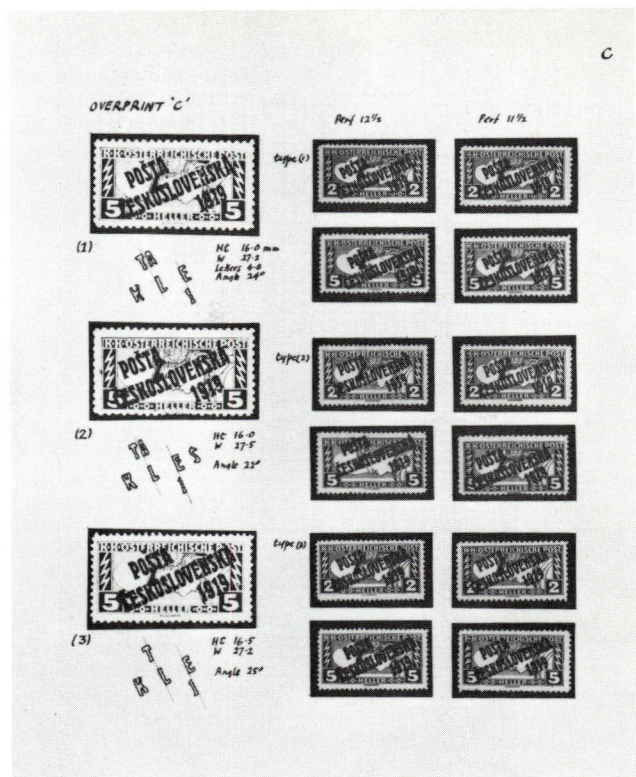

Photographs (as the three on the left-hand side of this page) help convey information without extensive writing-up. Modest enlargements of the whole stamp or greater enlargements of part of the stamp can be used. But here again it is important to give the stamps priority.

Although postal history has always been an element in collecting, it has recently attracted a very much larger following. Because the increase in interest is recent, this class of collecting is not always understood. What distinguishes a postal history collection from one in the general class is less the type of material displayed than the attitude of the collector. The collector must evaluate his material historically, which implies, among other things, paying attention to detail, and asking himself of every piece, Why? At what time? For what reason? In the context of what other events? The fact that all the stamps in a collection are cancelled and on envelopes does not make the collection postal history. Some connection must be established between the pieces and, ideally, not merely hinted at but developed and illustrated.

The F.I.P. defines a postal history collection as one 'based on the study and classification of postal and philatelic items which are directly relevant to the methods, routing and conditions of despatch of postal communications of all periods, or to the organisation to this end of postal services, whether governmental, local or private.' This definition is further amplified by saying that the collection will primarily be of used covers, adhesive postage stamps, and postal documents used to illustrate a postal historical theme; examples of such a theme will include pre-adhesive postal services, military mail, railway mail, censorship of mail and many other similar themes. The collection may contain *where strictly necessary* also stamps and their forerunners, maps, decrees and the like.

It is possible to think of an exhibit in the general class with scarcely any writing-up at all. It is impossible to think of one in the postal history section. Postal history demands writing-up; the problem is to make the text clear and concise; leaving out an important indication may be as bad as putting in too much. It is often much more difficult to fit a postal history theme into a given number of pages than an ordinary stamp exhibit. An extra small series of stamps can be squeezed into a page to condense an exhibit which is taking up too many sheets, but it is usually impossible to squeeze in an extra cover. It is essential therefore that written notes of the projected content of every sheet of the exhibit are prepared before a single cover is affixed to an album page.

The postal historian who has started this Guide by glancing at this chapter is asked to read the earlier chapters on collections in the general class and their presentation since almost everything said there applies also to the postal history collection and often with greater force. Some problems are more acute. For instance maps and supporting material are often essential (if they are not they are best left out). The problem is to avoid overloading the collection so that it becomes a scrapbook. Maps should be simple and if possible specially drawn so that only the significant places are marked (including a major city if the area is not immediately identifiable). In a stamp collection catalogue numbers under each stamp, as explained earlier, are not welcome; in a postal history collection identification of markings by reference to a standard text can be helpful and is to be encouraged. Since explanation may have to be extensive, the write-up underneath a cover may appear formidable, so it is worth considering whether some of the information cannot be neatly written in alongside or above, e.g. an observation such as 'Accountancy mark 15'. However if the account-

ancy mark is less than might be expected because, say, the letter is understamped and the receiving country will collect part of its share in postage due, this will have to be dealt with below since the explanation is unlikely to fit in sensibly alongside.

Supporting material is often of great interest to the public although its inclusion may be considered unnecessary by the jury. It is often sensible to prepare extra 'a' numbered pages which can be slipped into position if the exhibit is shown later at less formal exhibitions. On these pages it may be interesting to include, say, a photostat of the *Illustrated London News* picture of the wreck to give emotional impact to the wreck cover displayed austerely on its own on the page before.

The inclusion of stamps in a postal history collection was once considered wrong by some specialists. I believe that it is now generally agreed that stamps with clear postmarks can provide useful illustrations of a theme as well as giving variety to what would otherwise just be a succession of envelopes.

Collectors who have little experience of historical studies should be reminded that the inclusion of an instruction in a P.O. regulation does not mean that anyone ever followed it and that, if time allows, it is worthwhile checking the references of even the most prestigious authorities and re-reading the documentation for oneself. Frequent repetition sometimes gives inaccurate information the false colour of authority. A mistake in the writing-up will always cause an exhibit to be marked down; a new discovery, particularly the correction of a previous accepted error, will be rewarded.

Aerophilatelic Exhibits

Although no schedule of marking is provided by the F.I.P. rules for exhibits in the general or in the postal history class, there is a detailed schedule included in the rules for aerophilately. The attention of the jury is drawn to the following table:

1. Presentation, general impression	10
2. Philatelic knowledge and research	25
3. Development and extent of the collection	25

4. Historical, postal and aerophilatelic knowledge		15
5. Rarity of items		20
6. Special characteristics		5
		100

The two British national exhibitions adopt slightly different approaches. One gives the same schedule of marking as is allotted to collections in the general class; the other adopts a schedule which differs slightly from that of its general class in giving a few more marks for rarity.

	A	B
B1. Aerophilatelic knowledge and personal study	30	30
B2. Importance of exhibit, items exhibited and special features	30	20
B3. Rarity		15
B4. Condition	20	15
B5. Presentation	20	20
	100	100

The lack of agreement between the different standards is curious. The F.I.P. attaches little importance to presentation. Exhibition A adopts the same schedule as for the general class when it would be more logical to follow that of the postal history class. Exhibitors are always wise to study the rules for the particular exhibition which they are entering. Those who wish to plan their pages more generally will, I believe, be wiser to plan them as if aerophilately was a special branch of postal history, since this is exactly what it is. This means they will be right to include stamps as well as flown covers if they have been issued specially for the air post. It would be appropriate, say, if they annotated the various issues in terms of the air tariffs in force at the appropriate times. It would not, in my judgment, be appropriate to include in a collection submitted in the aerophilatelic class a display of plating a stamp which happened to be an air stamp. A study of this sort would belong to the general section.

The air mail collector is exposed to the temptation of allowing his pages to become a scrapbook, particularly if he has early material. Early photographs of planes and pilots, have great appeal. If excerpts from the pilots' logs have been published there is a temptation to turn the exhibit into a handbook. As in the preparation of all exhibits the exhibitor's judgment is under test. The test is rather more severe for the air mail exhibitor. I believe that it is right to include rather fuller information for the earlier flights when the type of plane and time taken is more significant than it may perhaps be later. For the earlier flights a brief indication of route may also be important. Beyond these observations it is difficult to go without being dogmatic. The reader is referred back to the earlier chapters, particularly those on presentation and postal history.

Thematic and Subject Exhibits

It is, I believe, easier for the collector of postal history or the owner of a single country collection to raise his pages to exhibition level than it is for the thematic collector. The traditional collector has at his disposal catalogues which not only determine what should be included but also in what order the material may be shown and from whom it may be obtained. The gap between the accumulation of stamps which depict animals (for example) and a thematic arrangement of the material worthy of being exhibited is considerable. Some help is obtainable from books which specialise in thematic and subject collecting, but much information must be obtained from those devoted not to stamps but to the subject or theme which stamps are to be used to illustrate.

The thematic class includes exhibits of two types, those which are properly described as thematic and those which are subject collections. The distinction will be discussed later. For the moment these general remarks about thematic exhibits refer to both types of exhibit.

Throughout the Guide emphasis has been laid on the logical unity which can be given to exhibits if stamps and covers are considered in the context of the social history of the postal services and not just as bits of paper which inevitably follow the sequence of catalogue numbers. Unless the theme chosen happens to be the social history of the postal service this aspect is insignificant in thematic collecting. Here the logical development arises not from the stamps but from the theme which might be 'Parasites' or 'Polo'. The philatelic material is used, often wittily, to illustrate the theme in ways in which the artist designing it and the authority issuing it would never have considered.

The thematic exhibit is like an essay. It will be judged by its style and by the novelty and elegance of its presentation and by the strength of its argument. In an essay on 'Friendship' the

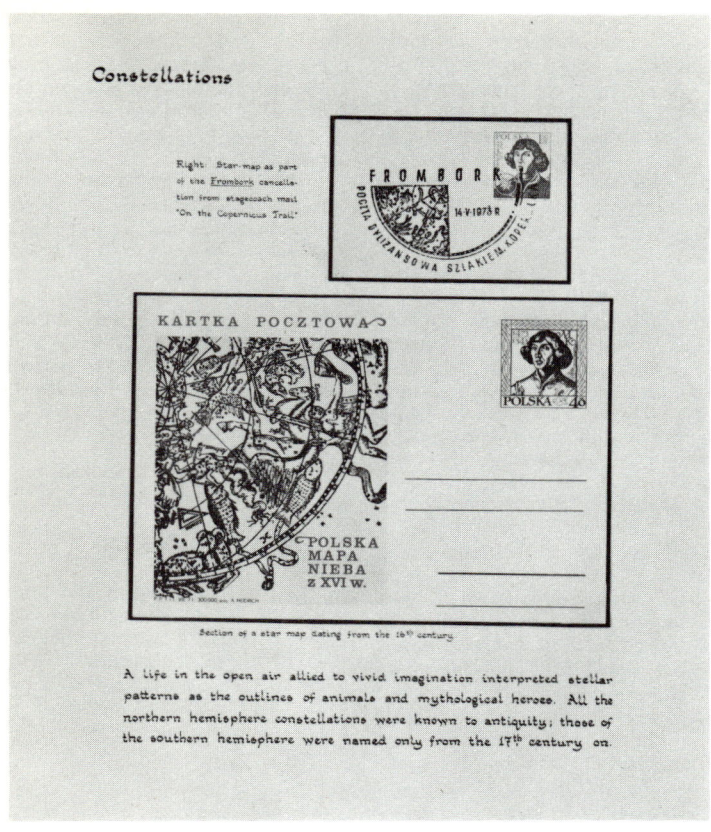

Constellations

Right: Star-map as part of the Frombork cancellation from stagecoach mail "On the Copernicus Trail"

KARTKA POCZTOWA

POLSKA
MAPA
NIEBA
z XVI w.

Section of a star map dating from the 16th century

A life in the open air allied to vivid imagination interpreted stellar patterns as the outlines of animals and mythological heroes. All the northern hemisphere constellations were known to antiquity; those of the southern hemisphere were named only from the 17th century on.

From a thematic collection of Astronomy. The commemorative postmark is displayed through a neat rectangle cut in the album page, a sensible method of showing two covers or cards without encumbering the page or cutting up one of them.

reader will expect new ideas, new metaphors and similes; he will not expect to hear again of Damon and Pythias and David and Jonathan. Because the style of the presentation is very important particular attention must be paid to the condition of the material and to the way that it is composed on the page. Illustrated postmarks should be clear and clean and although merit will always be given to the exhibitor who is able to find commercially used material in good condition, the jury in this class are likely to be more tolerant of the first day and special issue

cover which has been neatly cancelled specially for the collector and handed directly to him.

A quality of particular importance in a thematic exhibit is balance. The display will normally be divided into sections, the theme should be planned and the sections chosen so that the material is evenly distributed with no one section outweighing the other. If this appears not to be working out, the collector should rethink the title, either of the whole display or of the sections, so that balance is achieved. The same balance is demanded on the page, which will usually have to accommodate both stamps and covers. It is quite wrong to relegate covers and postmark material to a last chapter where it is all presented together. It should be distributed appropriately through the sections. It may be necessary for reasons of space to show some postmarks only on piece.

The analogy of an essay has already been used; it should perhaps be amplified so that the thematic exhibit is compared to a book divided into sections, chapters and paragraphs. All thematic collections, as will be explained when the F.I.P. rules are outlined later, must be preceded by album pages which outline the plan of the exhibit or collection section by section and chapter by chapter.

Since some exhibitors seem unaware of the distinction between a thematic and a subject collection, this should now be made clear. References in brackets are to articles in the F.I.P. regulations. The thematic class includes collections of two types, those that are properly thematic and those which are more precisely called subject collections. In a thematic collection the theme takes precedence and the stamps (please consider this single word to include covers, postal documents, postmarks etc.) are used only as illustrations. If the theme were 'Man's Inhumanity' there might be sections devoted to political persecution, religious persecution, racial persecution, economic persecution and stamps would be arranged in these sections regardless of issuing country. The designers of the stamps need never have thought of them in the context in which they are displayed in a thematic collection. For instance an old sailing ship might have been part of a series of old ships yet be included in the theme instanced above because it was known to have been a slaveship.

A subject collection includes all stamps which have a close relation with a particular subject or purpose of issue. The subject may be animals, Olympic Games, Rotary, Council of Europe, etc. The subject collection can be arranged in systematic order, in thematic order, by country or by date order. Many judges however dislike a mixture of methods within sections but accept differences between sections. For instance (Art 6.3.) a subject collection devoted to the Olympic Games may start with a thematic section devoted to the history of the games followed by chronological sections devoted to successive Olympiads.

The same subject can be treated as a subject or as a theme. If 'Animals' are treated as a subject stamps showing them might be arranged country by country and the collection would exhibit the different attitudes of national designers to the incorporation of pictures of animals on stamps. On the other hand the stamps could be arranged regardless of country, date of issue, etc. in zoological groups. If this method is chosen it is probably preferable to keep the arrangement within the groups thematic and scientific and not to change within the groups to arrangement by country of issue. The treatment of animals becomes more clearly thematic if the title is narrowed, as it has been in a famous collection, to 'Zoological curiosities' with sections treating anatomical strangeness, strangeness of bearing, incompatibility with environment.

Study of the F.I.P. recommendations for marking provides a useful guide to what is expected.

Thematic collections:
1. Presentation and general impression   10
2. *Theme*
  2.1 Plan of the collection and development of the theme 20 ⎫
  2.2 Originality of theme and exploitation of its potential 25 ⎬ 50
  2.3 Extent of the collection 5 ⎭
3. *Philatelic elements*
  3.1 Philatelic knowledge 15 ⎫
  3.2 Condition and rarity of stamps and documents 25 ⎬ 40
                              —
                              100

Subject collections:
1. Presentation and general impression   10
2. *Subject*
  2.1 Systematic study and extent of collection 25 ⎫
  2.2 Exploitations of subject's potential 15 ⎬ 40
3. *Philatelic elements*
  3.1 Philatelic knowledge 20 ⎫
  3.2 Condition and rarity of stamps and documents 30 ⎬ 50
                              —
                              100

The two British national exhibitions agree on the marking for the thematic class; no distinction is made here between thematic exhibits and subject exhibits.

Constellations

The northern celestial hemisphere appears on the above stamp, the outer circle indicating the celestial equator. The Milky Way is also shown.

Pegasus is a useful guide to other constellations.

The "Great Square of Pegasus" is easily located.

Ursa Major, Auriga, Hyades, Southern Cross.

The Zodiacal Constellations

Capricornus   Sagittarius   Virgo   Leo [and Sextans].

In the course of one year, the Sun appears to move slowly eastward in a path known as the Ecliptic. A narrow band on either side of this is called the Zodiac and is divided into twelve sections, or "signs". The Zodiacal Constellations were named in ancient times.

From the same Astronomy collection as the example on page 27. Noteworthy is the ordered and logical distribution of emphasis by the three sizes of lettering and the restrained use of underlining. The major emphasis remains rightly with the stamps.

1. Presentation	15	
2. Development of exhibit	25	
3. Scope of exhibit	15	55
4. Originality of theme	15	
5. Philatelic elements		
5.1 Knowledge	10	
5.2 Presence of philatelic items, including rare stamps and their condition	20	30
	100	

The British national marking penalises subject collections because these cannot be given marks for originality. The F.I.P. marking compensates for this by making the top mark for philatelic elements 10 points higher for subject collections than for thematic ones. This is probably logical since proofs and varieties of this sort are more appropriate to a subject collection.

This point is emphasised in a note to the F.I.P. rules (Art 6.4.). 'In a subject collection the essential point is assembling all the philatelic items. This is why, whilst taking account of the picture on the stamp or the purpose of its issue, a deeper study can be made of certain areas or . . . varieties. It is important, however, not to lose sight of the general idea of the collection.' In the thematic exhibit the originality of the theme and the wit shown in its deployment are vital. The unexpected yet apposite gives great pleasure. 'The collection should be sufficiently detailed to show personal character' (Art 3). The choice of material as well as the choice of theme should be original and unexpected. Stamps are not designed to illustrate botanical textbooks anymore than musical instruments are designed to imitate the cries of animals but with skill and wit they can both be used for these purposes.

There are some general points which will apply to both types of thematic exhibits. They will be improved by the variety of the philatelic material. The collector's knowledge will be demonstrated if covers, postal stationery, postmarks etc. are all used in illustration. Illustrations which are non-philatelic such as illustrated postcards should be avoided even if they have been given a temporary philatelic status by being sent through the post. Since modern stamps are easier to find than old, the jury will appreciate the presence of material from all periods. The album leaves should be of a quiet neutral tone. A modest symbol of the theme is permitted in one corner, but a thematic collection is not an excuse, as it is sometimes taken to be, for bravura writing up which reduces the impact of the stamps. Uniformity of presentation and writing-up throughout all the sheets is important and the presence of used and unused stamps in isolation on the same page is to be avoided. In both thematic and subject exhibits, but particularly in subject exhibits, brief philatelic notes can be put alongside the stamp or cover if there is something of interest to report and the general development of the exhibit is not interrupted.

As already observed, the exhibit in the thematic section has to be planned right through before the first stamp is placed on the page. This planning will be reflected in the text of the introductory pages which serves as the list of contents does in a book. It will show into what sections and chapters the display has been divided and give the number of sheets in each. Since, as the collection is improved, the number of pages in the chapters may be increased, it is prudent to enter the number of pages in pencil. Then alterations can be made without sacrificing the original pages. Since only a small part of an advanced collection can be displayed, it is usual to show the 'list of contents' complete but add a short note to say that for this exhibition selections have been made from pages in, say, sections 1 and 3.

The Jury and the Award of Medals

Since there might be some danger at international exhibitions of the jurymen being influenced by national pride in favour of their own countrymen, the F.I.P. have determined rules for their selection. The country in which the exhibition is held has the right to choose 25% of the jury from its own nationals and to complement these with a further 50% chosen from foreigners with specialist knowledge. Among these 50% no country may have more than two jurors and each should have a different speciality. The remaining 25% of the jury is chosen by the executive of the F.I.P. in consultation with the organising committee of the exhibition. The jury members select their own president and one or two vice presidents as well as a secretary. The members are then divided into groups with appropriate knowledge to judge the different sections of the exhibition. The groups have the right to decide for themselves awards up to and including vermeil medals. Higher awards have to be discussed by the full jury. All voting is by simple majority.

Juries for national exhibitions are chosen by the organisers who themselves appoint the chairman. The juries are similarly divided into groups according to specialities and the groups report their verdicts to the chairman who usually briefly checks every exhibit to satisfy himself that there is consistency of marking. He will discuss points of conflict with the various groups.

The level of marking which justifies a particular medal varies between national and international exhibitions. The lowest points for qualification are:

	International	National
Gold, large	95	—
Gold	90	85-90
Vermeil (Silver Gilt)	85	80
Silver	75	70
Bronze Silver	70	60-65
Bronze	60	50-55
Diploma	50	40-45

In theory, since a silver medal in a national exhibition is necessary to allow an exhibitor to enter an exhibit internationally and since there should often only be a 5% difference between national and international marking, a diploma should not be a possible award in an international exhibition. In practice silver medallists in national exhibitions often get bronzes when they compete internationally, i.e. they are marked not five points more strictly but ten.

Since an exhibit is not an exam with one word yes-or-no answers, the list of marks is just an indication. I think that the mind of the juryman often works in these stages. After the first survey of the exhibit he decides that it should qualify for a silver medal (this on the basis of his experience of other exhibitions). He then begins to assess the collection according to the criteria established for the section in which it is being judged. If he finds he is getting too low a total mark he asks himself whether he has not, at first glance, overestimated the virtues of the collection. If he finds he has not, he must check once more the marks allotted against the different criteria.

This point is made to emphasise the importance of the first impression. An outstanding presentation, a good range and variety of material, a new field interestingly and concisely written up will all make a good impression. A bad impression will be made by careless spelling (I have even seen an exhibit with the name of the country spelt wrongly!), cover after cover which look almost the same and only differ in small detail, or a collection which is trotted out without change exhibition after exhibition. There comes a time when judges begin to mark down a collection which has become too familiar so it loses a grade rather than gains one.

Juries are human and in planning an exhibit it is often helpful not to plan on general principles, but to think of a particular informed collector and arrange the sheets and write up in the way most likely to convey the message to him or her.

The field of collecting grows wider each year and exhibitors are ever seeking out new specialisations. The knowledge of judges will not always be able to keep pace. However this may be there is always an element of luck. The sensible exhibitor welcomes the opportunity of having his favourite sheets on show and knows that the metal of the medal is less important than the game and the pleasure of conversation with the other players.

How to Enter Exhibits

Two national exhibitions are held in Britain each year, Stampex (usually in February) and the British Philatelic Exhibition (in October). Collectors who wish to enter should apply to the organisers for a prospectus. Entry forms have to be submitted some two months before and the exhibits about a month and a half before the date of the exhibition. The size of frame and the number of sheets likely to be displayed vary between the two exhibitions. Collectors who wish to be sure of getting a full number of sheets displayed will prefer the British Philatelic Exhibition. Careful reading of the prospectus is very important, so application should be made for it early on so that it is received as soon as it is available and its instructions taken into account when preparing the exhibit.

Exhibitors who qualify for a silver medal in a national exhibition can submit their collection for exhibition internationally. They should make application for entrance forms and particulars through the national commissioner for Great Britain appointed by the organisers. The commissioner can often arrange for the transport of the exhibit to the exhibition. Enquiries made to the commissioner should be accompanied by the courtesy of a stamped and addressed envelope.

For particulars of forthcoming exhibitions intending exhibitors should refer to the philatelic press. If the name of the national commissioner is not mentioned in the press an enquiry should be made through the British Philatelic Federation. The instructions for packing, presentation, size of sheet and insurance should be studied carefully.

The first step to success in national and later international exhibitions is membership of a local philatelic society and, if possible, of a specialist society within the field of the collector's interest. From these he will not only get information and help but often also the opportunity of exhibiting parts of his collection before a friendly group whose praise and criticism will usually be stimulating. The B.P.F. Directory, published annually, will give the addresses of such societies.

Acknowledgment

The author would like to thank Mrs. Margaret Morris for kindly providing two pages from her thematic collection for the illustrations on pages 27 and 29.